W9-DDG-345

101
Budget Britain
Travel Tips

Other Books by Anglotopia

101 London Travel Tips
Great Britons: 50 Greatest British Historical Figures
101 UK Culture Tips (summer 2021)

Other Books by Jonathan Thomas

Anglotopia's Guide to British Slang
Adventures in Anglotopia
Anglophile Vignettes

101 Budget Britain Travel Tips

By
Anglotopia

Anglotopia Press - An Imprint of Anglotopia LLC
www.anglotopia.press

Printed in the United States of America

2nd US Edition: April 2021

Published by Anglotopia Press, an imprint of Anglotopia LLC. The Anglotopia Press Name and Logo is a trademark of Anglotopia LLC.

Print Book interior design by Jonathan Thomas, all fonts used with license.

All photographs © Jonathan Thomas

ISBN: 978-1-955273-00-8

Table of Contents

Introduction...8
1. How to Set a Realistic Budget...11
2. Beware of Bank Holiday Weekends...13
3. Watch out for Half-Term..15
4. Protect Your Trip with Travel Insurance...16
5. Top 5 Free Things to do in Lincoln, England......................................17
6. Top 5 Free Things to do in Norwich, England.....................................18
7. Book your Flights on a Wednesday...19
8. Travel with a Carry-On Bag Only...20
9. Amazon.co.uk is Your Friend..21
10. The Cheapest Way to get to Central London......................................22
11. Get an Oyster Card or Go Contactless..23
12. Where to Get a Free Maps..24
13. Save Money with Budget Flights Within Britain..................................25
14. Savings on Car Rentals...26
15. Getting a 'Free' Plane Ticket with Points? 30
16. Save Money on Train Travel in the UK..32
17. Save Money on Rail Fares - The Britrail Pass.....................................36
18. First Class Means FIRST CLASS in Britain..37
19. Skip the Train and Ride the Bus Instead..38
20. Always Use a Licensed Taxi - Not Just in London.................................39
21. Top 5 Free Things to do in Bath...40
22. Cash, ATMs, and Credit Card Fees..42
23. Watch out for the Congestion Charge in London..................................45
24. Bike Rentals from the Cycle Hire Scheme...46
25. Cross the Thames for Free..47
26. Just Walk to Save Some Money...48
27. Top 5 Free Things to do in Glasgow, Scotland....................................49
28. Top 5 Free Things to do in Cardiff, Wales...50
29. The Lowdown on Budget Hotels in Britain..51
30. The Cheapest, Cleanest Hotels in London? 53
31. Consider a B&B Over a Hotel...54
32. Hostels to Save Money in Britain..55
33. Live Like a Local with Airbnb..56
34. The Glories of Couchsurfing..57
35. Top 5 Free Things to do in Manchester, England.................................58
36. Top 5 Free Things to do in Liverpool, England...................................59
37. Find a Local Grocery Store or Snack Shop..60
38. Breakfast on the Cheap in London and Britain....................................61

39. Free Tea! 62
40. Why Not Share a Meal? 63
41. A Dirt Cheap Lunch – Ready-Made Sandwiches......................64
42. To Save Money - Just Don't Tip at all in Britain.......................65
43. Fast Food is Your Friend - No Shame in McDonald's................66
44. Don't Wait to Eat at the Airport...67
45. Top 5 Free Things to do in Bristol, England..........................68
46. Top 5 Free Things to do in Nottingham, England.....................69
47. Top 5 Tourist Attractions to Avoid in London.........................70
48. Just What are 'Concessions' Anyway? 72
49. Budget Tip: Don't Forget Your Student ID.............................73
50. Tourist Information Centres...74
51. How to See Britain's Cathedrals for Free..............................75
52. Free Fun: London's Parks..76
53. Join the National Trust for to Thousands of Properties.............77
54. English Heritage Overseas Visitor Pass................................78
55. The Telly is Free Entertainment...79
56. Take a Cheap Cruise on the Thames with the Tate-to-Tate..........80
57. Get 2-for-1 Entry to Britain's Attractions.............................81
58. The Cheapest Bus Tour in London - The Heritage Line..............82
59. Free British Audio Tours - Rick Steves' Audio Europe App...........83
60. Consider the London Pass for Savings in London.....................84
61. Cheap London Guided Walks...85
62. Top 5 Free Things to do in Birmingham, England.....................86
63. Top 5 Free Things to do in Newcastle, England.......................87
64. Where to Get Half Price Theatre Tickets in London..................88
65. Best Places in London to Hear Free Music.............................89
66. People Watching is Free! 90
67. Read Local British Newspapers to Discover...........................91
68. Book a Dinner and Theatre Combo Deal................................92
69. Top 5 Free Things to do in Leicester, England........................93
70. Top 5 Free Things to do in Aberdeen, Scotland.......................94
71. Pay Attention to your Coins...95
72. Buying Souvenirs on the Cheap..96
73. Don't Buy British DVDs – They Won't Work at Home................97
74. Don't Convert to Dollars at Checkout..................................98
75. Hold on to Your Receipts for a VAT Refund at the Airport...........100
76. Consider Joining Historic Royal Palaces................................101
77. Shop at Local Markets - Avoid Touristy Markets......................102
78. Candy Makes a Great Souvenir for Family Back Home...............103
79. British Books on a Budget? Try Used Bookstores.....................104
80. What About Budget Transatlantic Airlines? 105

81. Duty-Free Shopping at the Airport..106
82. Top 5 Free Things to do in Edinburgh, Scotland.....................107
83. Top 5 Free Things to do in Brighton, England.......................108
84. Top 5 Free Things to Do in Belfast, Northern Ireland..............109
85. Cheap Phone Calls Home...110
86. Saving on Taxis in London and Beyond.................................111
87. Smartphone Tips...112
88. You Don't Need a Passport Cover...113
89. Don't Waste Your Money on a Travel Voltage Converter..........114
90. Don't Waste Money on Airplane Chargers...............................115
91. Top 5 Free Things to do in Coventry, England.........................116
92. Top 5 Free Things to do in Bournemouth, England..................117
93. 5 Free Things to do in Cumbria..118
94. Don't Be Afraid to Buy it There...120
95. Don't Carry all of your Money with You...................................122
96. Stock up on Camera Memory Cards and Batteries..................123
97. How to Find Free Public Toilets in Britain................................124
98. How About Avoiding London All Together? 125
99. Top 5 Free Things to do in Plymouth, England.........................126
100. Top 5 Free Things to do in Dover, England.............................127
101. Don't Forget to Have Fun! 128
About Anglotopia...131

Introduction to the 2nd Edition

Much has changed since we wrote the first edition of 101 Budget Britain Travel Tips almost ten years ago. We have changed. Travel has changed (and I don't just mean because of COVID-19). And Britain has changed.

So, rewriting this book was quite a challenge. I had to scrap about a quarter of the original tips because they weren't relevant or the advice was no longer any good.

Also, the way we personally travel has changed quite a bit. When we first started Anglotopia in 2007 we were 'new adults' just out of college, so our travel was based on saving as much money as possible just so we could go to Britain. While we still try to travel frugally these days, we've also had a lot of experience of the pitfalls of sticking to the cheapest options possible. Our focus on travel now is to save money where we can, but also to be willing to spend a little extra where it counts so we make the most of our trips to Britain.

Still, there are many things that we Anglophiles can do to save on travel in the United Kingdom, and there are still 101 good tips in this book to help you (and I'm sure we could find 101 more!). But the best thing you can do is to pick and choose the things that matter to you most so that you can get maximum enjoyment for what you're willing to spend.

It's still unclear what will change with travel in the UK after the COVID-19 pandemic is over. And much WILL change. There will be fewer attractions to visit, but there will also be plenty of new opportunities from the ashes as people seek to start new travel-related businesses and take advantage of a resurgent market. The desire for people to visit the UK hasn't disappeared because of the pandemic, so when it's over, there will be a recovery; it might be slow at first, but it will rebound. I can't be the only one with a trip planned and ready to go as soon as it's safe and acceptable to travel.

The ethos behind this book is reflected in how we produced it. We want the book to be as affordable as possible - there's no point in charging a high price for a book that is supposed to save you money! So, unlike the other books in this series, there are no color pictures to reduce printing costs and the page count so we can offer a low price. We hope this compact little book will help you build the knowledge to have affordable and enjoyable trips to Britain.

Jonathan & Jacqueline Thomas
Publishers
Anglotopia

I.

How to Set a Realistic Budget for your Trip to Great Britain

The number one thing you can do to ensure that your trip goes smoothly is to plan ahead well in advance. Everything from where you are going to stay to what you are going to eat to what you are going to see – it all starts in the planning stages. When thinking about all of this, it is really important to start with the money you plan to spend and what will come out of these funds. For example, will your hotel bill come out of this, or will that be paid ahead of time?

As you are planning the days of your trip, do some research. Many attractions and sites are free in England, such as most museums. Some attractions, such as the Tower of London and other historical palaces, are not free. If you are staying in London, keep in mind that it is one of the priciest cities in the world. That does not mean that it can't be done on a budget; you just really need to plan ahead. Once you know the cost of the attractions, set a loose itinerary and see how much it will cost you to see what you want to see.

Along with seeing the sights, you are going to have to plan how you will get to those sights. It is awesome if you are within walking distance, but what if you aren't? You can make your way around most cities cheaply using public transportation. Do some research here. A lot of public transportation systems offer some sort of multiple ride program, and this may save you a lot of money. Another good thing to know is when does public transport run? On one of my first trips abroad, I had a very early train to catch. I went to jump on the Tube in London only to see that it was closed! In those days, the Tube didn't run 24 hours a day - nowadays some lines do. I ended up having to take a cab, which was an unexpected expense. So, always check the hours of the train/Tube lines you need to use.

One of the most important things in your budget is food. I have found myself thinking "If I only eat one meal a day or just snack throughout the day, I will have more money to see things." In my experience, this is a huge mistake. You need to eat well. Set a realistic budget for food. A good hearty breakfast is a necessity, and also plan for a light lunch and a big dinner. The cheapest way to eat is to get a takeaway sandwich and a packet of crisps or buy fast food (you can eat a whole meal from McDonald's for under £5). Do not deprive yourself of food money for other things. You will end up hungry and feeling lousy. You want to be in top shape to see the sites because there is often a lot of walking involved. Make sure to stay hydrated too!

Last but not least, make sure to leave a little "cushion" of funds for the unexpected. It really is a good idea to have some emergency funds should you need them for any reason. Make sure you can access these funds while you are abroad if necessary. They won't do you much good if you can't get to them. A credit card with some available credit is handy for this.

Another word of caution here is to be street smart when trying to cut costs. For instance, never take an unlicensed taxi-cab in the hopes of getting a better deal. You won't!

Remember: Plan an itinerary deciding what you want to see, research entrance fees for attractions and the cost of transportation to get there and set a good meal plan for yourself. With a little bit of planning and forethought, you can have a wonderful time on your vacation abroad.

Based on our experience, a good estimate for a trip to Britain centered on London is about $3,000- 4,000 USD for a single person — for a about a week and add a couple of grand if there's two of you or a small family. You can do it for less, but that all depends on how much you want to suffer.

2. Beware of Bank Holiday Weekends

I f you're going to be in Britain on a bank holiday weekend, be prepared for things to be closed, to close early, be crowded, and also to be more expensive.

A bank holiday is a public holiday in Britain where most of the country is off work – that is, except for people who work in tourist hotspots. It can also be more expensive to travel on those weekends as you'll have to share attractions, lodging, airplanes, and the roads with other Brits – which means prices will be higher as they are peak travel times. This also means that anything free will be crowded with Brits in search of cheap things to do on a bank holiday!

While most museums and major attractions will be open, they usually keep special holiday hours (often the same as Sunday hours).

Here's a list of the usual bank holidays so you can avoid them:

- New Year's Day
- Good Friday
- Easter Monday
- May Bank Holiday (first week of May)
- Spring Bank Holiday (first week of June)
- Summer Bank Holiday (last Monday in August)
- Christmas Day
- Boxing Day

Some of the holidays will vary on their observance between Wales, Scotland, and Northern Ireland. Also, if a bank holiday is on a weekend, a 'substitute' weekday becomes a bank holiday, usually the following Monday. Check locally or Gov.uk for the latest dates.

3. Watch out for Half-Term

Britain's schoolkids usually get a one-week break in the middle of their semesters, and this time off is called half-term. This means that Britain's popular tourist attractions will be mobbed with kids and families as they seek to take advantage of the days off. Free attractions will be especially mobbed. We've seen lines stretching around blocks in London with people waiting to get in - just because it was half-term and they were free.

While you'll have to contend with more crowds, keep a lookout for special half-term deals. Many of the railways, museums, and other attractions will offer special half-term deals – even if you're from outside the country. Many will do a two-for-one deal or offer kids entry for free.

When is half-term time in Britain? That will depend on which part of Britain you're in, but here's a rough guide:

- Autumn term: Early September to mid-December (half term: late October)
- Spring Term: Early January to Easter (half term: mid-February)
- Summer Term: Easter to mid-July (half term: late May/early June)

4. Protect Your Trip with Travel Insurance

Bad things happen. Flights get canceled. Hotels get overbooked. Natural disasters happen. Pandemics spread worldwide. While it's an added cost to your trip, you may want to consider getting some type of travel insurance.

Our biggest reason for recommending this is that if something happens and the onus isn't on your airline or hotel to fix the problem, you have to fix it yourself. If you're on a budget, how can you afford to get yourself out of a sticky situation?

You can expect to spend $100-200 per person for good travel insurance. It's worth the peace of mind. While it's uncommon for American tourists to buy travel insurance, peace of mind is priceless (though look at reviews for GOOD travel insurance, you don't want to be fighting with someone on the phone in a foreign country).

5. Top 5 Free Things to do in Lincoln

Lincoln is most famous for its stunning cathedral, but there's plenty of other things to see and do that won't break the pocketbook. Here's our list of free things to do:

- **Lincoln Cathedral** - You can enter free of charge and gaze at the nave, spend time in the quiet Morning Chapel, or visit the shop. There is an admission charge for the rest of the cathedral.
- **The Collection** - Visitors to historic Lincoln can enjoy a fabulous free-to-enter museum and the region's premier art gallery, the Usher.
- **Museum of Lincolnshire Life** - Enjoy free entry to the largest and most diverse community museum in Lincolnshire.
- **Battle of Britain Memorial Flight Visitor Centre** - While a little far out of town, you can explore Britain's rich aviation heritage here. There is a charge for guided tours of the collection.
- **Explore Canals** - Explore Lincoln's beautiful canals.

6.

Top 5 Free Things to do in Norwich

Norwich is a lovely town near the North Sea that has many exciting attractions to visit. We've put together a list of our favorite free things to do:

- **The Old Skating Rink Gallery** - The South Asian Decorative Arts and Crafts Collection (SADACC) presents its extensive collection of the everyday arts, crafts, and cultures of South Asia in this gallery, only 50 meters from the Forum in Norwich.
- **Norwich Cathedral** – This magnificent Romanesque Cathedral is open all day to visitors of all faiths and none. Set in beautiful grounds, it is an awe-inspiring and welcoming building. With spectacular architecture, magnificent art, and fascinating history, it is well worth a visit.
- **The Forum** - This is a stunning community building in the city center and is the ideal place to meet any time of the year.
- **Sainsbury Centre for Visual Arts** - This inspirational public art museum at the University of East Anglia (UEA) is a short distance from Norwich city center.
- **The Assembly House** - In the heart of the city, this fine Georgian historic house is a leading venue for the arts, concerts, exhibitions, and meetings.

7. Book your Flights on a Wednesday

When it comes to booking your airfare to Britain, there are a few things you can do to save some money. Here's our biggest suggestion: fly on a Wednesday.

Mid-week airfares are almost always lower than traveling on the weekend. You can also save money by flying on a Tuesday or a Thursday but, usually, Wednesday is the cheapest day to fly to Britain.

British Airways has a great booking system that lets you see the airfare for each day of the week around your preferred date. This is an incredibly useful tool.

It can be inconvenient workwise to book a vacation leaving mid-week, but you'll definitely save some money this way. This applies to coming home too - if you plan to come home on a Wednesday, airfares will also be cheaper.

8. Travel with a Carry-On Bag Only

It's no secret that airlines are trying to get every last penny they can get out of travelers, and one of their most innovative ways is to charge for your checked bags. Well, the joke's on them, because if you pack cannily, all you'll need is a carry-on bag for your trip. This is a great way to save money while flying to Britain. You'll also get through the airport much faster, as you won't have to wait for baggage reclaim.

The other passengers may hate you as your bag will take up more space in the overhead bin, but these days it's every traveler for himself!

The only problem with this plan is that, most likely, you will return with more than you left with in souvenirs and other purchases. Consider shipping those home or checking a souvenir-only bag on your return trip. Memories cost nothing while souvenirs do twice – when you buy them and when you have to try and get them home!

Beware the 'budget' transatlantic carriers that have popped up in recent years. While they have rock-bottom airfares to Britain, they charge for everything, including carry-on bags. As I'm writing this during the COVID-19 pandemic, it's not clear if any of the budget transatlantic carriers will survive but, if any do, they will return to their old tricks of charging for everything.

9. Amazon.co.uk is Your Friend

We've all been there – you've arrived in Britain, and you forgot something. This causes two problems – you have to find the item and go buy it, and you have to pay money you didn't budget for the item. This has happened to us a few times over the years, and the 'easy' solution (other than going without) is to buy something on Amazon.co.uk.

They will usually have the cheapest prices on most things. And Britain is a small island; even if you're not a Prime member, most items will be delivered to you the next day after they ship. So, like me once, if you forgot a camera battery, you can just buy it on Amazon and have it delivered to your hotel, B&B, or self-catering property.

There are, of course, other online retailers in Britain, but Amazon is the biggest with the largest selection. Start there; if you can't find it, just search for it on Google, and you'll find what you need.

Or call a local shop and go on an adventure to find the needed item!

10. The Cheapest Way to get to Central London from Heathrow

Well, walk. Just kidding! The most affordable way to get into central London from Heathrow Airport is to simply take the London Underground. You can take the Piccadilly Line from Heathrow straight into central London for the cost of a cup of coffee. It will take about 40 minutes or so and can be inconvenient with luggage, but this is the cheapest way bar walking. Buses (also called coaches in Britain) are another way to get into central London cheaply. But the bus will take the longest time.

11. Get an Oyster Card or Go Contactless

For the cheapest Tube fares in London, you must get an Oyster Card or set up contactless payments with your Credit Card. An Oyster Card is a travel card that you load money on to travel the Tube and bus networks. Using the Oyster Card, you can save **50-60%** on your Tube fare compared to paying cash. No matter how much you travel in a day, you'll always be charged the lowest possible fare, and paying with an Oyster Card is usually much cheaper than purchasing a day or week pass.

You can easily purchase them before you leave for London from Visit Britain Direct: http://www.visitbritaindirect.com/ or you can also buy one at many shops or Tube stations.

If your credit card offers contactless (aka tapping), then you can also use it at the gates on the London Underground without even buying a ticket or an Oyster card. You'll be charged at the end of the day based on how much you travel and how far you go. It's very easy to do!

12. Where to Get a Free Tube Map and Free Tourist Maps

One of our favorite things to do is just look at the London Underground network map. We even used to have one on our wall as a poster. Having a copy of the map in your pocket is indispensable while in London as it's great to look at whenever you need it.

So, where can you get a Tube Map for free?

Well, first, you can get a free network map at pretty much any Tube station on the network. We recommend searching one out at the airport, so you have it for your whole trip.

Second, you can get one in a tourist information office, they are dotted all around central London (but watch out for booking services looking to take your money).

Alternatively, you can print your own copy by downloading the latest version from Transport for London at https://tfl.gov.uk/

TFL also makes a great Tube app for mobile phones that has the map and route planning; it's completely free. Just search your mobile App Store for the Tube map.

You can also get free railway network maps or line maps at the railway stations. I do love pouring over railway maps and timetables…

Bonus tip: Most local tourist authorities will send you free brochures and maps if you simply ask for them! They're a great resource for planning trips and all the information is free – they'll also answer any questions you may have about any given area.

13. Save Money with Budget Flights Within Britain

Easyjet and Ryanair offer cheap fares all around the British Isles, and it's a great way to fly to Edinburgh, Belfast, or Dublin if you're on a budget. You can sometimes get a ticket for as little as £20.

But be warned, these airlines are the worst at charging extra fees that can end up making the journey cost more. If you're canny and avoid the fees, you can save a lot of money traveling this way.

Easyjet: http://www.easyjet.com/

Ryanair: http://www.ryanair.com/

They're also great airlines to fly with if you want to leave Britain and explore Europe. You can cheaply fly to most European cities for pennies. But pay attention to the airport they actually fly to - often they are far away from the cities you're trying to get to!

14. Savings on Car Rentals

Hiring a car can be a great way to get around Britain - you're not beholden to the train schedules, and you can go anywhere or see anything that can be reached by car. But renting a car can be very expensive. Here are a few quick tips to save on a car rental in Britain.

1. Book Far in Advance

Book your car rental (or car hire as they say in Britain) far in advance. This will get you the best rate you can get. The closer you get to your trip, the more it will cost. It also pays to check multiple websites and booking systems to get the cheapest rate.

2. Pay in Advance

Many car rental places will offer you the chance to pay for your entire rental in advance. This will usually save you 10 or 20% on your total rental. A lot can go wrong from the time you book to the time you go, so I generally avoid paying for something in advance. But if you're willing to take the risk, you'll save money.

3. Don't Pay for Excess Insurance

The car rental company will try to sell you extra insurance. You don't need this. Especially if you've booked with a valid credit card, as most credit cards support car rental excess (check before you go). If you refuse to pay for the car rental company's insurance, expect them to confirm that your card has it.

Your rental quote will normally include basic coverage, including third-party coverage, vehicle damage coverage, collision damage insurance, and vehicle theft coverage. This is all that's required by law in the UK. The rest is a risk you can take. Your credit card may also cover beyond the minimums.

We fell for the car rental insurance scam when we rented a car for the first time, and it almost doubled the cost of our car rental. We're not doing that again.

4. Learn to Drive a Manual

Manual transmission cars are the standard in Britain and how most Brits learn to drive. So, most rental cars have a manual transmission. Renting an automatic transmission car is 'exotic,' so the rates for those are often double what a manual car is. So, if you know how to drive a stick, you can save quite a bit on your rental!

5. Don't buy petrol at motorway services (or pay for their gas)

Supply and demand. It makes the world go around. This also means that, when you buy gas at a convenient location on a motorway services stop, you will pay a premium on petrol (as they call it). Petrol in Britain is very expensive, so saving just a few pence per liter can lead to big savings. Get gas at smaller gas stations or along your journey, don't do it at the motorway services. There are phone apps that will show you the cheapest gas around you.

6. Return it to where you rented it from

It's best practice to return your rental car to the same place that you rented it from. For example, if you got it at Heathrow, return it there. Otherwise, they will charge you a hefty fee to return it somewhere else. We like to return ours in central London for convenience reasons, but this adds like £50 to the bill because you have to pay extra fees and pay London car taxes.

7. Don't hire a car GPS

I can't believe the car rental places are still pushing GPS units for your car when everyone has a phone that has free GPS and mapping. As long as you have an international data plan for your mobile, you absolutely don't need a GPS system from the car rental place. A printed road atlas is way cheaper and more fun to navigate with!

8. Have airline miles?

Have you accrued a ton of airline miles and can't use them all on free plane tickets? Most will let you redeem them for car rentals. This makes it essentially free, though there may still be a fee or two depending on the car rental company. I recently used all my miles for a free car rental, and it was worth it!

9. Book the smallest car possible

In addition to booking a manual car, if you also book the smallest car possible, you'll save loads of money. This can get tricky if you're traveling as a family, as you may not have room for all your luggage. But if you're on your own or just with a partner, then you only need two seats and a steering wheel!

10. Stick with one driver

The car rental company will be happy to put your partner or spouse on the car rental so you can both drive the car. But they will charge you through the nose and, depending on your age, this can double your rental cost. If one of you is fine doing all the driving, then stick with that.

15. Getting a 'Free' Plane Ticket with Points?

It's possible to book a trip to Britain - including airfare and hotel and hire car, without paying a dime. Welcome to the world of credit card points gaming. I've never been a big fan of this method for various reasons - mostly being I don't like to use Credit Cards for much of anything.

But yes, if you have a miles or points credit card, you can accrue miles or points that you can then use to book travel. Your mileage will vary (see what I did there?) based on the airline's rewards programs and the credit card. If you're canny, though, you can essentially travel for free - assuming you don't travel that often.

Some points games are simply games - like if you use the British Airways credit card and accrue Avios miles. BA charges you the full taxes and fees when you book a rewards flight - so essentially you can only save a few hundred dollars rather than travel for free. But if you are a member of another airline's program and accrue the miles, they may not charge you taxes and fees at all, and you can get a free ticket, assuming you can get one of the free rewards seats for when you want to go.

I'm simplifying something that can be overly complicated. And that's by design; they don't WANT you to redeem your miles, so they make it very difficult. But if you play the game right, you can get rewards like a free plane ticket to Britain.

Personally, since we prefer to just fly BA everywhere, we've never had a free flight going to Britain. BUT, since BA is in alliance with American Airlines and owns Aer Lingus, you can use your points on those airlines and save quite a bit. For example, I save my BA Avios miles to pretty much fly domestically for free within the USA (usually only costs $5 plus the miles). I also flew to Ireland for $150 once, using my Avios miles (you have to call to book this). I've also used my Avios to pay for car rentals or get a discount on hotels.

So, while sometimes it might not be worth using airline miles for booking a plane ticket to Britain, there are other ways to use them to save money.

But, as all of this requires the frequent use of a credit card, beware that you can easily get into trouble if you overspend or an event happens that makes you lose your income.

16. Save Money on Train Travel in the UK

Britain invented the idea of the railways, so it makes sense that they have one of the most well-developed train networks in the world. You can get to most places in the UK by train and, if the train doesn't go there, you can at least get pretty near it. Britain's rail network is geared towards commuters - even in the cities outside of London - they exist to feed people from Britain's suburbs into the cities for work. That said, intercity train travel is still very important, and it can cater well to a tourist. Here's how.

Understand Fares

There are four main types of tickets on the British rail system. The most expensive and most flexible tickets are called Anytime tickets. This ticket type lets you travel on any train, at a fixed price, and can be bought right up to when the train leaves. The cheaper option is called an Advance ticket, where you have to book in advance and travel on a specific train (sometimes an 'open' ticket - sometimes not - meaning you can travel at any time). Then there are the Off-Peak and Super Off-Peak tickets – these ticket types are advance tickets that are available outside peak times (more on that later).

Single vs. Returns

Sometimes when you book a train ticket, it can be cheaper to book two separate 'single' (one way) tickets rather than a return ticket that includes both journeys. There's no difference in the journey other than that you will have two separate tickets (hold onto them!).

Split Ticketing

One strange quirk of the UK train system is that it is sometimes cheaper to buy two separate tickets for different sections of the same journey – and you don't even need to change trains. It works best for longer journeys and more expensive tickets - like traveling from London to Manchester or York, etc. Or when you need to travel at peak times or at short notice. Here's an example: say you were going from London to York on a weekday morning, it would cost you £200. But by buying separate tickets from London to Manchester and then from Manchester to York you could save loads of money, and you can sometimes stay in the same seat. There's a free online tool called Split Ticketing that helps you work out the best place to split your journey and shows you whether it'll save you money.

Off-peak Travel

This is by far the best way to save on train fares in Britain. As I said, the network is designed now for commuters - so they use the system mostly in the early morning and the late afternoon. If you can reserve your journey for after the commuter hours (usually after 9:30 am or so and before 4 pm or so), then you can save quite a bit of money - and also crucially have more room on the train as it won't be as crowded.

Book in Advance (but sometimes the day before)

Booking far in advance is also a great way to save money on tickets. Much like booking a plane ticket, booking your train ticket far in advance can allow you to save money. The downside to this is most train franchises won't let you book more than 90 days in advance (there are exceptions).

Use an App

There are ample apps to help you book your trip - most of the train franchise operators have their own. But I recommend getting the Trainline app, as it will aggregate all the train operators in one place and give you the cheapest options for tickets. They also support e-tickets, split ticketing, and you can track train times and journeys right from the app. You will pay a small booking fee if you use the app, but it's worth it because the app can save you money overall. That said, if a train journey is particularly expensive, check with multiple sources to make sure you get the best price.

Consider Railcards

See if you qualify for a railcard. They're discount cards that allow you to save quite a bit on train fares if you meet the requirements. If you're under 26, for example, you can save 1/3 off your bookings. International travelers can get them. Check the railcards website for details and eligibility: https://www.railcard.co.uk/

Consider Railpasses

Railpasses are only available outside the UK for use within the UK (Brits cannot get them). But basically, you pay a flat fee for unlimited travel on Britain's rail network for a certain amount of time (with caveats, of course). If you plan to make your entire journey around Britain by rail, this can be a great way to save loads on fares as you pay for them in advance and then don't have to worry about it. The only downside is that if you travel much less than you planned you will have wasted the money.

Use the train as a free hotel!

You can save on a night's hotel if you book one of Britain's night sleeper trains. The Caledonian Sleeper goes nightly from London to Scotland (and vice versa), and the Night Riviera goes from London to Penzance (Cornwall) and vice versa. If you book a berth/room, you combine the cost of the journey and a night's hotel. We've done this - and it's a lot of fun. If you think you can sleep on a moving train, that is.

17. Save Money on Rail Fares - The Britrail Pass

The Britrail Pass is something that's only available to those who live outside Britain. It's a pass that basically gives you unlimited travel on Britain's rail network for a set period of time.

They can be expensive but, if you plan to do extensive travel on Britain's rail networks, they can pay for themselves very quickly.

You have to buy your pass before you arrive in Britain as you cannot buy them there (wouldn't want the Brits to get these great deals, would we?)

More info: https://www.britrail.com/

18. First Class Means FIRST CLASS in Britain

One of the weird things to get used to in Britain is that their classes of travel are very rigid. Many trains - even commuter trains - have first-class cabins, which is rather strange in itself.

Unless you have a first-class ticket, you cannot go into the first-class cabin, even if it's empty. If you're caught, you could be forced to pay an on-the-spot fine or have to buy a full fare first-class ticket. Rest assured, your ticket will be checked by the conductor.

First-class tickets on short journeys don't usually cost much more than regular tickets so, if you want a little more legroom and a quieter ride, consider traveling first class. Just don't consider trying to do it for free.

What do you get in First Class on Britain's rails? Extra legroom, usually leather chairs. Sockets for plugging in your computer. Sometimes a meal or a better meal service. But it really depends on the journey. The experience in First Class from London to Birmingham will be much different than London to Scotland!

19. Skip the Train and Ride the Bus Instead

I f you want to get around Britain cheaply, there's another option that doesn't get as much attention as Britain's trains: the bus (or the coach, as they say in Britain).

Britain has a vast intercity bus network, and you can get around Britain very cheaply this way. For example, you can get from London to Edinburgh for under £50 if you book far enough in advance (try finding train fares that cheap - you won't!).

You may groan at the idea of spending a couple of days on a bus, but you probably shouldn't. Remember, Britain is a small country, and you can drive between most major cities within a day or less. The bus trip from London to Edinburgh is just 9 hours, for example.

If you can handle the swaying of the buses and want to see Britain's motorways instead of its railways, give the bus a try.

We recommend looking at Megabus first:
http://uk.megabus.com/

20. Always Use a Licensed Taxi - Not Just in London

Wherever you are in Britain and need to use a taxi, always use a licensed service. Never use a mini-cab or other unlicensed service.

It's a safety issue and a cost issue.

Licensed taxi services have to give you the best fare to your destination, and they're heavily regulated because of this. They also have to be trained in their local area on where everything is (in London they call this "The Knowledge").

Mini-cabs and other unlicensed cabs aren't held to the same standards, and they can charge whatever fares they want. It's also very unsafe to ride in an unlicensed taxi.

If you need to take a taxi, always be on the lookout for a licensed cab. In major cities, this will be obvious. In smaller towns, you might have to ask, but your safety and pocketbook are worth it.

Since we originally wrote this guidebook, Uber and other ride-sharing apps have completely upended the taxi industry in Britain. You can usually book a ride via one of the apps for much cheaper than you would by booking one over the phone. The apps are where it's at now, but using Uber has its own risks/rewards. Just be careful.

21. Top 5 Free Things to do in Bath

Bath is understandably one of the top destinations for American tourists in Britain. The popularity of Jane Austen, the presence of Georgian architecture, and the ease of getting there from London make it a guaranteed stop for most Americans. As Bath is a tourist hotspot it has prices to match. Here's a guide to a few free things there to save you a few pennies.

1. Royal Victoria Park - Opened in 1830 by the 11-year-old Princess Victoria seven years before her ascension to the throne and was the first park to carry her name. The park is overlooked by the Royal Crescent and consists of 57 acres with attractions that include a skateboard ramp, tennis, bowling, and putting green and 12- and 18-hole golf course, open-air concerts, a large children's play area, and a 9-acre botanical garden. Seasonal attractions include carnival fairs and hosted events.

2. Royal Crescent - One of the most famous street scenes in Britain, these elegant Georgian townhouses dominate views in

Bath (and in recent British TV shows like Bridgerton). Enjoying the park in front and the views around it are free. The museum at the end of the terrace is not, however (though worth visiting).

3. Pulteney Bridge - This iconic bridge is like a mini-London Bridge with shops and flats that span the River Avon. It's a beautiful setting and enjoying the sublime beauty of it is absolutely free!

4. Holburne Museum - The city's first public art gallery, the Grade I listed building is home to fine and decorative arts built around the collection of Sir William Holburne (nothing to do with the musician). Artists in the collection include Gainsborough, Guardi, Stubbs, Ramsay, and Zoffany. Well worth a visit!

5. Bath Abbey - Admission to the abbey is technically free, though they funnel people through an area that looks like a ticket area and have a suggested donation. This is actually optional (though if you're going to enjoy the place, why not donate?). If you enter through the shop, you can avoid awkwardly telling the person you don't want to donate. It's free to have a wander around. And, like most churches and cathedrals in Britain, it's free to come to worship.

22. Cash, ATMs, and Credit Card Fees

Traveller's cheques are firmly a thing of the past. I don't know anyone who can still use them. The best way to get cash 'on the ground' in the UK is to simply use an ATM. When you use an ATM, you get the best possible exchange rate. And while your local US bank may charge you a fee, most ATMs in the UK are free at the point of use. We bank personally with HSBC, which is Britain's biggest bank and they have branches in the USA - this gets us free ATM access in the UK, so we don't have any fees at all when we use an ATM (but, as of this writing, it looks like HSBC is getting out of the US market, so this may change).

In most major banks in the USA, you can usually get foreign currency like British Pounds, but I do not recommend doing this. There are fees for this and the exchange rate is not great. Same goes for exchanging your money at an airport - never do this - the currency exchanges in airports are designed to fleece you for the most amount possible and the rates are awful. Just use a bloody ATM as soon as you get off the airplane - there will be plenty of ATMs in the airport terminal to get the cash you need to get your trip started.

That being said, cash is on the wayside in the UK like it is everywhere else. 2020 and the COVID-19 pandemic practically killed the use of cash - simply because paper money is filthy. Most people now use their credit cards or Apple Pay/Google Pay with their phones. Many have gone contactless, which most US credit cards now offer. In the UK, it's very rare to sign for a credit card transaction as now are mostly chip & pin, which the US has also started to transition to.

You also need to watch out for transaction fees for foreign purchases. For example, my local business bank here in Indiana charges a percentage fee on foreign transactions. This can add up to a lot when you have dozens of charges on a trip (and if you use it to book a hotel... then look forward to triple digit fees). So, check your credit/debit card terms and conditions to make sure you don't have these fees. While I'm not a huge fan of credit cards, finding a card just for travel that does not have these fees is a good idea. For example, I have a British Airways Credit Card that does not charge these fees at all and is great for travel. If you want a debit card that does not charge travel fees, then consider the PayPal Debit Card, they do not charge fees either and you can simply load money into your PayPal account for your trip.

The 'best' deal you can manage is to spend local currency in Britain - having your own British pounds bank account and debit card. This used to be almost impossible unless you were very wealthy. Enter Transferwise onto the scene (which as of Spring 2021 was rebranding to Wise). They're a decentralized currency exchange platform that has the best exchange rates and crucially they let you have a free virtual bank account in dozens of currencies - like British Pounds and Euros. They now also have a debit card, that will allow you to spend that currency when you're traveling - and the card is free and having a balance is free. You can also use the card at ATMs and get local pounds in cash without fees.

Now, on our travels, I load up the account with British Pounds (you can transfer in from your US bank account at the current market rate - like you get at an ATM) and then when we're in the UK, we can spend our pounds like a local with the Wise debit card. It's all very slick and innovative and cuts down substantially on various foreign transactions. If you're going to be a frequent traveler to the UK I highly recommend signing up for this as it's completely free. If you run low on funds, simply open the Wise app on your phone and load up the account with more pounds from your US bank. It's seamless and wonderful. If you plan to visit Continental Europe or Ireland on your trip you can set aside money in a Euro account with Wise and spend like a local there as well.

Travelex has a similar product called the Cash Passport, but it's not nearly as good and is comparatively expensive, because their exchange rates are terrible and they have loads of fees.

Stuff happens! That's why you should absolutely not rely on just one method of payment for your trip. If your card is declined or worse - it gets stolen - you will need another way to pay for things. So, have several credit cards and don't carry them all with you at one time. Save your bank's phone number in your phone in case you need their help in an emergency. Don't put all your eggs in one basket, as they say!

And finally, it's absolutely necessary to warn your bank that you will be traveling abroad. You want to avoid the embarrassment of having your card declined because your bank flagged your purchases abroad as potential fraud because you didn't tell them in advance. Most big banks will let you do this online. If you bank at a local bank or credit union, just give them a call. You'll have to provide your exact dates of travel and then you should not have any issues.

23. Watch out for the Congestion Charge in London

Several years ago, a fee was introduced in central London for all cars that enter the congestion charge zone. If a car enters the zone, it has to pay a toll of £10 during the week during daylight hours (weekends and holidays, there is no charge).

It's supposed to reduce traffic in Central London. As tourists, we haven't really noticed much of a difference in traffic, and it really seems like more of a cash grab for the London government.

That said, even if you're renting a car, you are still responsible for paying the charge. If you don't, you could end up with the charge on your car rental bill with some added penalties from the car rental company (especially if you don't pay it on time).

So, if you drive your rental into London, go online and pay your charge right away. We've heard horror stories of travelers who got huge bills from their rental company for forgetting (or just not knowing).

Congestion Charge:
https://www.tfl.gov.uk/roadusers/congestioncharging/

24. Bike Rentals from the Cycle Hire Scheme

I f you want a really cheap way to get around London, consider renting a bike from the Santander Cycle Hire Scheme. The bikes are located all around London, and anyone can register to rent a bike. You ride it to the next station to return it. It's a great way to see London on a bike – if you're brave enough to face London's clogged and dangerous streets.

Another bonus: it's cheaper than a taxi!

You can sign up online to access the system, or you can pay for your rental on the spot at the bike terminals. It costs £1 to access the system; then you're charged £1 for the first hour. The first 30 minutes are free, so all you pay is the access fee if your trip takes under 30 minutes. It's a great deal. You can get to a lot of places in central London in 30 minutes.

Check the website for more details: https://tfl.gov.uk/modes/cycling/santander-cycles

There are now also cycle hire schemes in other major British cities, that operate on a similar principle. Check with the local tourist authority.

25. Cross the Thames for Free in the Greenwich Foot Tunnels

If you want a fun experience and don't want to pay to cross the Thames into Greenwich on the Tube, consider using the free Victorian-era foot tunnels that cross under the river.

The Greenwich Foot Tunnel is a pedestrian tunnel under the Thames that runs between Greenwich and Island Gardens on the other side. There are about a hundred steps at each end, but it's free and open 24 hours a day. The tunnel just went through a refurbishment, and there are new elevators if you don't want to brave the stairs.

The Woolwich Foot Tunnel is a crossing under the River Thames in East London from Woolwich in the London Borough of Greenwich to North Woolwich in the London Borough of Newham. There are currently no lifts while the tunnel is being renovated.

There's also a free ferry you can take called the Woolwich Free Ferry.

We've done this one, and it was a lot of fun!

26. Just Walk to Save Some Money

This tip is for London in particular: consider walking to your destination instead of taking public transportation. London is a big city and has plenty of options for inexpensive transportation, but sometimes it is just nicer to walk. I am speaking particularly of the Tube. While it is fast and inexpensive, it is almost entirely underground in London. You miss so many of the sights traveling completely underground.

The Tube maps show the location of stations slightly skewed. Some are actually quite close together, and you can easily walk between them. However, stations with many connections, like Bank, are so large that you might not want to walk. Either way, walking the streets of London allows you to really see the city. Who knows what gems you might uncover on a stroll.

If you get a bit lost, don't panic. Have a good pocket map with you (or mobile app), and you can always politely ask a passerby for directions to where you are going. Make some time to walk above ground while you are in London because there is a lot to miss if you stay underground the entire time.

27. Top 5 Free Things to do in Glasgow

Glasgow is Scotland's largest city, and it's recently gone through a bit of a renaissance. There's much to see and do culturally, and we've put together a list of the top 5 free things to do:

- **Riverside Museum of Transport** - This dynamic new museum displays Glasgow's rich industrial heritage, which stems from the River Clyde. A Tall Ship is berthed alongside the museum, creating a fantastic experience in this stunning setting.
- **St Mungo Museum of Religious Art** - This award-winning museum is a haven of tranquility in a bustling city. Its galleries are full of displays, artifacts, and stunning works of art. They explore the importance of religion in people's lives across the world and across time.
- **Kelvingrove Art Gallery and Museum** - This is one of Scotland's most popular free attractions. Kelvingrove has 22 themed, state-of-the-art galleries displaying an astonishing 8,000 objects.
- **Gallery of Modern Art** - As the center for Glasgow's modern art collection, its changing displays are inspired by what the city owns.
- **Glasgow Cathedral** - The first stone-built cathedral was dedicated in the presence of King David I in 1136. The present building was consecrated in 1197. Since that same period, the cathedral has never been unroofed, and the worship of God has been carried out within its walls for more than 800 years.

28. Top 5 Free Things to do in Cardiff

Cardiff is one of Britain's most vibrant capital cities and recently invested millions in turning around its seafront. There's much to see and do these days, and we've put together a list of the top 5 free things you can do:

- **The National Museum & Gallery, Cardiff** - History, science and the arts at your fingertips, the museum & gallery really captures your imagination. It houses the best collection of Impressionist paintings outside Paris. Stroll through elegant art galleries housing world-famous works of art or take a journey back in time to explore a land of dinosaurs and woolly mammoths.
- **The National Assembly for Wales Visitors Centre** - You can learn more about Wales and Cardiff itself at the Pierhead and Cardiff Bay Visitors Centre.
- **St Fagan's National History Museum** - Located 4 miles west of the city center on the grounds of St Fagan's Castle, this is one of Europe's foremost open-air museums representing the life and culture of Wales. Situated in 100 acres of parkland, the museum also has displays of costumes, daily life, and farming implements.
- **Bay Art Gallery** - The gallery on Bute Street promotes major exhibitions by Welsh and international artists.
- **Cardiff Summer Festival** - one of the UK's largest free festivals.

29. The Lowdown on Budget Hotels in Britain

One of the biggest costs of any trip is lodging. Hotel prices in the UK can be outrageous! You can find a great deal on a nice hotel, but there are some pitfalls to avoid. Here are a few tips on budget lodging in the UK.

Check the Neighborhood - Yes, you may have found a super nice hotel for a great price but, if the price seems too good to be true, it probably is! This is pretty common. The neighborhood may not be necessarily a "bad" area – it may be too far out, too. You will not save any money staying outside of the city center, because you are going to spend more, in the long run, commuting back and forth. Speaking from experience, commuting back and forth from the hotel is a real bummer.

Read Reviews - We always read reviews before we stay anywhere, no matter the price point. You have to read reviews with a critical eye. Some people are really finicky about certain things and can give a hotel a bad score unnecessarily. There are only two things that will put us off in reviews – bed bugs and dirty rooms. However, we have to see this type of complaint more than once in many reviews before we take it to heart.

When to Check Out - If you get to your hotel, and it is downright scary, don't immediately panic. You got a good deal on the room for a reason. The questions to ask yourself are: Will I be safe here? Is the room too dirty? Are there bedbugs?

Rude Staff - A British friend and I were talking a while back, and we joked that in the United States, the customer is always right, and in the UK, the customer is always wrong. Rude staff isn't always the case, but we have pretty much come to expect it. This is not a reason to leave your hotel. Just try to be polite and go your own way.

Not all budget lodging is scary - Honestly, we have only had one less than desirable experience while staying in the UK; the room was dirty, and the hotel was noisy. We stayed there for the duration of the trip because we didn't spend a lot of time in the room. That is the moral of the story here: you didn't travel abroad to spend all of your time in your room. Get out and see what you came to see. You simply need somewhere to sleep and wash in a safe environment. Read reviews and do your homework before you stay, and you will do okay.

30. What are the Cheapest, Cleanest Hotels in London?

The cheapest and cleanest hotels in London are the EasyHotel chain of hotels located in South Kensington, Paddington, Victoria, Heathrow, Earl's Court, Luton, The City, and various other locations.

Rooms are very basic, offering just a bed and a bathroom. There are no amenities, and you even have to pay for the privilege of watching the TV. However, rooms are clean, comfortable, and in safe neighborhoods.

Rates start at £25 a night if you book far enough in advance, which is a great deal for London!

We have found, though, that the cheaper a hotel gets in London, the more likely you are to not want to stay there. There are plenty of scary looking hotels outside of central London catering to those you… would not want to stay around. A policy of local councils is to place people who can't live anywhere else in small hotels and B&Bs. While most of these people are perfectly lovely, it might not be the right kind of place for a tourist.

31. Consider a B&B Over a Hotel

I f you're looking to save money on lodging in the UK, you might want to consider staying in a bed and breakfast. You get to stay with locals, get that personal connection, and breakfast is included. In rural areas of Britain that aren't well-served by hotels, B&Bs are a great alternative.

We've stayed in a few B&Bs. We have always enjoyed ourselves, and the pocket was hit a little less hard than if we stayed in a hotel. You won't save much if you stay in B&Bs in London, but elsewhere in Britain and in the countryside, you can save a lot.

But please check reviews and photos on sites like Tripadvisor. You do not want to find yourself in a flophouse as there are just as many crap B&Bs as there are good ones in Britain.

32. Consider Staying in a Hostel to Save Money in Britain

This option is more popular with students and younger people than more seasoned travelers, but you can save a lot of money by staying in a hostel instead of a hotel.

Staying in a hostel requires a little bit of sacrifice as you sometimes have to share a room – as well as a bathroom. The trade-off is that you get a cheap place to sleep, and you meet a lot of interesting people from around the world. You can find a bed as low as $10-20 a night.

If you do opt for a hostel, keep your wits about you and guard your valuables. There are people who prey on hostelers (seeing them as easy marks). As long as you watch out, you should be safe.

A good place to look for hostels:
https://www.hostelbookers.com/

33. Live Like a Local with Airbnb

Staying in a flat while traveling isn't a new travel trend, but Airbnb has totally changed things. Instead of only companies offering flats for let, people are now letting out rooms in their apartments or houses. You can also rent an entire property. It's a great way to cheaply rent a cottage in the countryside.

Prices can be pretty cheap depending on where you're willing to stay and what kind of accommodations you need. Availability will be strange and change every time you do a search so, if you see something you want, book it right away. They've got listings all over the UK, so you'll easily find something no matter where you want to travel in Britain.

Airbnb also has lots of safeguards built in so you don't end up with nowhere to stay if something goes wrong. If you want to make some money while you're in Britain, you can even rent out your own home while you're away.

Check it out: https://airbnb.com

Alternatively, there's also HolidayLettings.co.uk, which we've had good experiences with. There's also now a site called VRBO that does the same thing.

34. The Glories of Couchsurfing - Staying for Free in Britain

If you're really on a budget and basically want somewhere to stay for free while you're in Britain, consider joining the website Couchsurfing.org.

Couchsurfing is a travel social network where people offer their couches or spare beds to weary travelers for free. It's a way to grow your network of friends and gain a new experience.

We've heard a lot of good things about this method of travel, but it's not something we've ever done. With something like this, safety is paramount, so do be careful.

Website: https://www.couchsurfing.org/

35. Top 5 Free Things to do in Manchester

There are many attractions worth seeing in Manchester if you're on a budget. Here are our five favorite free attractions in England's industrial heartland of Manchester.

- **Manchester Town Hall** - A symbol of Victorian Age architecture, this building is a marvel to behold.
- **Manchester Cathedral** - Unlike some others in the UK, you don't have to pay to get in and have a look around.
- **Museum of Science and Industry** - Great museum dedicated to the industrial revolution with many exciting displays.
- **Manchester Art Gallery** - Great collection of British and European art that just reopened after a major renovation.
- **Castlefield Urban Heritage Park** - Great collection of buildings from a rebuilt Roman fort, world's oldest train station, first industrial canal, and much more!

36. Top 5 Free Things to do in Liverpool

L iverpool is one of Britain's biggest cities, and there is much for the tourist to do. Here are five free attractions:

- **Liverpool Cathedral** - Another of Britain's beautiful cathedrals that's free to enter and have a wander around.
- **Albert Dock** - Great area of regeneration with lots to see and do that doesn't cost a dime.
- **Tate Liverpool** - A lovely museum of contemporary and modern art in a fantastic setting.
- **Merseyside Maritime Museum** - Explore Liverpool's rich maritime history in this dedicated museum.
- **International Slavery Museum** - While the topic is not the most uplifting, explore the history of the modern age through slavery.

37. Find a Local Grocery Store or Snack Shop

If you are traveling on a budget, this tip is an absolute must. When you arrive or shortly thereafter, find a grocery store or corner shop that sells packaged food. Look for snacks like fruit, prepackaged crackers, or cookies. We highly recommend trying "crisps" what we call "chips." They come in some really interesting and amazingly delicious flavors.

We brought a box of cereal once and just ran to the local store for single pints of milk for breakfast. We ate cereal out of the teacups that were provided in our room, and we were even able to pick up a bunch of bananas to go with our cereal for a healthy and inexpensive breakfast.

You may even want to visit your local grocery store before you leave and bring some food home for snacks. Just make sure that whatever you bring is prepackaged and still sealed, or you will have trouble getting it through Customs.

If you are bringing food from home, just remember to avoid liquids. Food must be sealed in its original packaging, and you cannot bring in any fresh fruit or vegetables. If you are shopping while you are in the UK, remember you will most likely not have a means of refrigeration or a way to cook most food items. Check your hotel room first to see what you have available to you for cooking and storage purposes, then venture out to the store.

38. Breakfast on the Cheap in London and Britain

Eating out for breakfast in Britain can be very expensive. While there's nothing better than a good English fry-up, our top tip for getting breakfast on the cheap is to stock up on breakfast foods when you arrive.

When we hit a local grocery store, we always buy breakfast provisions for the trip, including bananas, muffins, bottled water, and any other food snacks that don't need to be cooked or refrigerated.

It's great. We have everything we need for a quick breakfast in the room so we can hit the ground running in the morning and be good until lunch. We usually spend £10-20 doing this, and we're good on breakfast for the whole trip!

39.

Free Tea!

Most hotel rooms will provide you with a tea kettle and tea. Take advantage of this before leaving your room rather than paying for a cuppa while you're out and about. Tea will be the lifeblood of your trip. Most will also include coffee on the tea tray.

40. Why Not Share a Meal?

A great way to save money for an expensive dinner out is to share a meal. Most food portions in Britain are bigger than one person can eat, so simply ask for an extra plate and split your plate with your travel partner.

Some restaurants may not allow this, so be sure to ask first.

To take the best advantage of this, order a starter, main course, and dessert and share them all. You'll have to eat the same thing as your partner, but you've saved the cost of two meals.

41.
A Dirt Cheap Lunch – Ready-Made Sandwiches

Britain invented the sandwich, and that's very clear in Britain today. Most convenience stores and food stores in places like railway stations stock a huge array of cheap, ready-made sandwiches. This is a great way to save money on lunch, and you can find them almost anywhere.

When we travel by train, we like to grab a sandwich at the station and then have an impromptu picnic. It's a hearty lunch, and you won't pay a fortune for it.

The big chain stores will have the cheapest sandwiches, but you can get higher-quality sandwiches at places like Au Bon Pain or EAT. Be sure to try some uniquely British sandwich combinations.

42.

To Save Money - Just Don't Tip at all in Britain

If you're traveling on a budget and concerned about your money while in Britain, consider just not tipping. Tipping isn't as commonplace in Britain as it is in the USA, and it's very difficult to judge when it's appropriate. No one will think any worse of you if you don't tip at all.

Most restaurants put a service charge in the bill already. For other services, if you're never going to see the person again, what does it matter if you don't tip them? However, if you will be utilizing a person's services again in the course of your trip, and they did a good job, it's not a bad idea to tip anyway. But for most situations, hold onto your pence; it's not expected of you anyway. We usually round-up to the next pound when tipping for taxi journeys.

43. Fast Food is Your Friend - No Shame in McDonald's

While it's not the healthiest way to eat while you're traveling, eating fast food while in Britain will save you a lot of money. You can usually eat a tasty and filling meal for under £5.

You benefit from not going into a restaurant with waiter service. You'll pay a premium for waiter service and most likely experience bad service anyway.

Whether it's going to McDonald's (which tastes better in Britain) or hitting up the local fish and chips shop, fast food is by far the most affordable way to eat in Britain.

44. Don't Wait to Eat at the Airport

This is more of a general budget traveling tip rather than one specifically for Britain, but it's simple: don't eat at airports.

Airports have captive customers, so prices don't have to be low. You'll even overpay at somewhere like McDonald's. To avoid high prices, either eat a good meal before you go to the airport or pack a lunch and eat it before you go through security.

We made the mistake of waiting to eat at the airport, and we were disappointed at how terrible the food was and shocked at how much we spent for the privilege to eat it.

45. Top 5 Free Things to do in Bristol

Bristol is a lovely seaside town on England's west coast, and there's much to see and do. Here's a list of five free things we discovered!

- **M Shed** - A former warehouse in Bristol's docks has been turned into a museum dedicated to its rich maritime history.
- **Bristol Museum & Art Gallery** – This museum and gallery tells the story of our world in every display – from the beginning of time to the present day.
- **Clifton Suspension Bridge** - The world-famous bridge was designed by the great Victorian engineer Isambard Kingdom Brunel.
- **Bristol Blue Glass Factory & Shop** – The factory and shop shows off the famous glassworks that have been synonymous with the city of Bristol for the past four centuries.
- **Bristol Cathedral** - A magnificent Gothic cathedral that dates back to the 1100s with free admission.

46. Top 5 Free Things to do in Nottingham

Nottingham is steeped in history, and that means there is plenty to do on a budget. Here's our list of free things you can do:

- **Green's Windmill and Science Centre** – This windmill in Sneinton was built by the father of notable scientist and mathematician George Green in 1807. Today the working mill is a popular museum and science center, which teaches new generations of children about the valuable work of George Green.
- **Wollaton Hall & Deer Park** - Wollaton Hall is a spectacular Elizabethan mansion in the heart of Nottingham. It is a prominent Grade One listed building, and visitors of all ages are welcome to visit the hall and park.
- **Angel Row Gallery** - This is a lively contemporary art gallery with a program of exhibitions that covers a whole range of art, including painting, photography, video, and installations.
- **Galleries of Justice Museum** - Based at Nottingham's old courthouse and jail, there are many ways to explore the museum with free exhibitions, audio & performance led tours, and a themed café.
- **Nottingham Contemporary** - Designed by the award-winning architects Caruso St John, this is one of the largest contemporary art centers in the UK. It has four galleries lit by 132 skylights, a performance and film space, and runs learning programs and varied events, including activities for families.

47. Top 5 Tourist Attractions to Avoid in London

London is a city wonderfully designed to take a tourist and part them from their money. While we get the appeal of more touristy attractions, London is not an amusement park. We prefer authentic history, actual history. That means generally avoiding places where people are in costume acting. Here's our list of overrated London attractions worth skipping due to cost and the crowds:

- **London Dungeon** - A place dedicated to celebrating torture and turning it into entertainment. Yes, the past was a terrible place, but you can learn those terrible things in a museum, not with a bunch of actors trying to make it entertaining.
- **Madame Tussaud's** - They practically invented the very idea of a tourist trap. Yet, this place endures, and there is always a line around the block of people trying to get in to see the life-size recreations of famous people. Worship at the altar of the celebrity here!
- **Buckingham Palace/Changing of the Guard** – Look,

it's a beautiful house, but it's closed to the public most of the year, the Queen is rarely there, preferring Windsor (which is more worth visiting), and the Changing of the Guard is a tourist mob.

- **Anything Jack the Ripper related** - Jack the Ripper has spawned an entire mini-industry in London for walking tours and even a new museum, but it's all rather distasteful when you consider that they all seek to entertain you about the deaths of a bunch of women who were gruesomely murdered. Hard pass.
- **The Sherlock Holmes Museum** - It's a museum dedicated to a person that never existed, in a place that never existed. Filled with dodgy looking mannequins and questions about history (and fiction), also there is always a line around the block. True Conan Doyle fans will be disappointed and will be a few pounds poorer.

48. Just What are 'Concessions' Anyway?

I n America, we're used to getting discounts for being part of some kind of group – be it a student discount or a senior discount. In the UK, they call them concessions.

When you see pricing for concessions, that means there is a special kind of discount with it - if you meet the requirements, you can get it.

Be prepared to prove it, though!

49. Budget Tip: Don't Forget Your Student ID

If you're still pretty young and held on to your Student ID from your college or high school days, then take it with you. Many paid tourist attractions offer student discounts.

The discount sometimes isn't much, but every penny helps in an expensive place like Britain. Most of the time you won't even have to show your ID but, if you do, it's nice to have it. Some attractions might require an International Student Card, but your school ID should suffice at most locations.

Keep in mind, though: some things, like train tickets, have an age limit on student fares, so this trick won't work there.

50. Free British Travel Resources: Tourist Information Centres

Britain has a huge network of Tourist Information Centres usually located in areas of interest to tourists. They're a great resource staffed by locals who know the most about their area.

You can usually pick up free local tourist materials, brochures, maps, etc. You can also ask the helpful people questions about travel in the area, and they'll be happy to help you out.

They're also able to help book local accommodation and give you advice on what to avoid. Just look out for their trademark signage or ask around in town. If you can find the phone number in advance, you can also call and get information over the phone to help you plan your trip in advance.

Many of these services have moved online and most local tourist authorities will have a website of some kind.

You can find a huge list of them here:
http://www.britainexpress.com/TIC/

51. How to See Britain's Cathedrals for Free - Attend Evensong Services

If you want to see the inside of Britain's famous cathedrals for free, all you need to do is wait until the tourist hours are over and attend an actual church service.

Choral Evensong is free, and you get to see the cathedral for free. After they close the cathedrals to tourists, you can still come in and watch the nightly service, usually held around 5 pm. You can probably even have a wander once services are over.

You get to hear beautiful music and then see the cathedral for free. You can't beat that, even if you're not religious. If you're in London, we recommend Westminster Abbey and St Paul's Cathedral. Outside London, we recommend Salisbury Cathedral, Durham Cathedral, and York Minster. Check with each cathedral as evening service times vary.

You'll have to put your camera away, though, as photography usually isn't allowed during services out of respect for worshippers.

52. Free Fun: London's Parks

We have traveled to London almost 20 times and have seen pretty much every attraction, paid and free. However, despite all of the amazing things we've seen, Hyde Park in London has to be practically our favorite place on the face of this Earth. London is full of free parks, squares, and gardens that are just as beautiful.

London's parks make a great place to visit. You can rest under a shady tree, take an awesome picnic, or just sit and people watch. Parks are also wonderful places to visit if you have children; ideal for letting them run off some energy.

Do a little research, and get yourself a good map of London. Most of the parks are open year-round, and they always have something new to see. Some attractions, like the Winter Wonder Fest in Hyde Park, aren't free, but there is so much more to see of the park that is free. Take some time, take a stroll, and really enjoy London's parks, squares, and gardens.

53.
Join the National Trust for Free Entry to Thousands of Properties

I f you intend to visit a lot of Britain's historic homes and castles, it may be wise to consider membership in the National Trust, which can get you free access to all their properties.

The National Trust is an organization that preserves Britain's heritage, and they own thousands of properties. If you're not a member, you have to pay for access to charging properties (like Churchill's House, Chartwell). These admissions can add up to quite a bit!

With a membership in the National Trust, access to all these properties is included. If you're an American, you need to join the Royal Oak Society, which is their sister organization in the USA. It costs just $55 per year for a membership, and it will pay for itself in one day of visits.

https://www.royal-oak.org

54. Consider Getting an English Heritage Overseas Visitor Pass

Like the National Trust, English Heritage runs hundreds of historic properties throughout the UK, some of which have pretty steep admission prices. Luckily for the overseas traveler, they offer an Overseas Visitor Pass that offers discounted entry into all their properties.

The Overseas Visitor Pass from English Heritage includes free entry to over 100 stately homes, castles, abbeys, Roman and prehistoric remains. With a pass, you can visit all attractions directly managed by English Heritage free of charge. It also includes free or reduced-price entry to hundreds of action-packed events, as well as a 290-page color souvenir guidebook containing maps, information on over 100 staffed attractions, and a further 300 free attractions in the care of English Heritage.

Prices start at £35 and vary based on the length of the trip. There are further options for families and children.

More info here:

https://www.english-heritage.org.uk/visit/overseas-visitors/

55.

The Telly is Free Entertainment

We love exploring everything that London has to offer a night, but that can get expensive really quickly. Dinners out, tickets to a show, transport to and from the hotel, etc., add up quickly. Most of the time, we're exhausted in the evenings anyway.

This makes watching British telly a free and easy way to enjoy some of the best bits of British culture without even having to leave your hotel room. Most hotels will have a TV with all the major networks. You can see what's going to be on in the daily paper or at www.radiotimes.com.

Some of our favorite memories of travel in London are eating a cheap takeaway meal in our hotel room watching British TV.

By all means, at least plan one or two special things in the evenings while you're in Britain, but there's no shame in having a relaxing evening in watching the telly. It's what the British are doing!

56. Take a Cheap Cruise on the Thames with the Tate-to-Tate

If you're looking for a great way to see London but don't want to pay for the high-priced boat tours, consider taking the Tate-to-Tate boat ride. It's an all-day boat service that runs from the Tate Modern to the Tate Britain and vice versa every 40 minutes during gallery opening hours. You'll get to see a huge chunk of London from the Thames, and you get the added bonus of visiting a great museum at the end.

It only costs £9 for one day (about $11 USD or so). It's even cheaper if you have an Oyster Card (which you should have!).

See website for current rates and timetables:
https://www.tate.org.uk/visit/tate-boat

57. Train Travel: Get 2-for-1 Entry to Britain's Attractions if You Travel by Train

Britain's rail operators have a great ongoing deal for passengers to get to Britain's top tourist attractions. They offer 2-for-1 entry if you use a train ticket.

They've got lots of fantastic 2-for-1 attraction offers and some great deals on train travel, including GroupSave, where 3 or 4 people can travel together Off-Peak for the price of 2 adults to hundreds of destinations!

Your first step is to browse the website and find the relevant attraction and related coupons. All you have to do is sign up on their website, fill in the details of your journey, and you'll get a voucher for use to get into the attraction. Easy as pie!

Days Out Guide Website:
https://www.daysoutguide.co.uk/

58. The Cheapest Bus Tour in London - The Heritage Line

Most of the classic London Double Decker Routemasters have been taken out of service, but they still run them on one bus line in Central London. This is a great way to get a bird's-eye tour of London for the cost of a single bus ticket – about £2.

The classic Routemasters runs on bus route #15. It's really affordable and fun to hop on, climb to the top, and ride the bus as it circles through all the London sights. It's also much less expensive than other bus "tours." You get the same treatment on any London double-decker bus, but Routemasters have a lot of history.

Carry a guidebook with you so you can read up on the landmarks you see or just sit back and enjoy the sights and sounds of London as they pass by below you.

59. Free British Audio Tours - Rick Steves' Audio Europe App

Rick Steves has released a great free app for travelers that's perfect for a trip to Britain. It features a ton of audio content that you can use for free.

The app includes segments from Rick's radio show as well as some of his classic walking tours. They make a great companion to his guidebooks.

Just for London alone, there are 12 walking tours in the app, and they're all FREE! There's also a great variety of audio for things to do beyond London.

I'm not sure why they're giving the app away as it's filled with tons of valuable content. The tours feature images to guide you around - really helpful.

You can download the app for iPhone or for Android, so there's wide platform availability. Rick also provides free maps you can download and print of the walking tour routes.

Download here:
https://www.ricksteves.com/watch-read-listen/audio/audio-europe

60. Consider the London Pass for Savings in London

The London Pass is a great way to save money on your next trip to London.

The Pass gives you free access to most of London's top tourist attractions so that your costs are fixed before you arrive. Conveniently, you can also get transport on the London Underground bundled into the card so you can save on getting around. Some of the attractions London Pass works with are actually already free – but you get added benefits such as free audio tours or guidebooks. With every purchase of a London Pass, you'll be given a great little guidebook that lists all the attractions and how to get to them. It might be a great buy that can save you money. Might is the key word there.

Our London Pass Recommendations:

- Buy it with transport included for added savings.
- Don't bother with a 1-day pass. It's not worth it as you won't have time to go to more than a couple of attractions in a day. Buy at least a 3-day pass.
- 6-day passes are the best deal all around and give you plenty of time.
- Some attractions they advertise are already free to get in, but having a pass gets you a benefit like an audio tour or free guidebook when you get there.
- Children may already be free at a lot of the attractions on the pass, so you might not need to buy them one.
- Buy several weeks before your planned trip.

61. Cheap London Guided Walks

If you're not careful, you'll end up paying an arm and a leg for a guided walking tour in London. Many people book guided tours through their airline or their hotel. Do not do this if you're on a budget, as you'll overpay.

We recommend London Walks instead – a company in London that's been around for a long time and offers a ton of different London walks at very affordable rates.

Their daily walks cost just £8, and you don't need to reserve a spot – just show up. Walks take about two hours and £8 is not bad for two hours of entertainment. They also offer day trips outside of London that cost £14 (plus train fare).

Here's a sampling of their London Walks:

- The Olympics Walks
- Ghost Walks
- Harry Potter Walk
- The Royal Wedding Walk
- And more!

Check their website for tours and times:
https://www.walks.com/

62. Top 5 Free Things to do in Birmingham

Birmingham has a rich industrial heritage, and there's much to see and do in one of England's biggest cities outside London. Here are our picks of the best free things to see and do:

- **Victoria Square** - One of the great public squares in Britain. Enjoy the fountains, people watching, and beautiful architecture.
- **Birmingham Museum and Art Gallery** - One of Britain's finest history and art museums. It has a collection of international importance covering fine art, ceramics, metalwork, jewelry, archaeology, ethnography, local history, and industrial history.
- **Weoley Castle** - The ruins at Weoley Castle are over 700 years old and are the remains of the moated medieval manor house that once stood here.
- **Ikon Gallery** - A world-class modern art gallery in the center of Birmingham.
- **Birmingham Cathedral** - The city's beautiful Baroque cathedral.

63. Top 5 Free Things to do in Newcastle

Newcastle is a fine northern city where there's plenty to see and do. We thought we'd put together a list of the top free things to see and do if you're on a budget:

- **BALTIC Centre for Contemporary Art** - Housed in a landmark industrial building on the south bank of the River Tyne in Gateshead, BALTIC is the biggest gallery of its kind in the world, presenting a dynamic, diverse and international program of contemporary visual art.
- **The Angel of the North** - The Gateshead Angel of the North is Britain's largest sculpture, designed by Antony Gormley for Gateshead Council. It weighs 200 tons, is 20m high, and has a 54m wingspan.
- **Great North Museum: Hancock** - Highlights of the new museum include a large-scale, interactive model of Hadrian's Wall, major new displays showing the wonder and diversity of the animal and plant kingdoms, spectacular objects from the Ancient Greeks and mummies from Ancient Egypt, a planetarium, a life-size T-Rex dinosaur skeleton and much more.
- **Church of St Nicolas** – a stunning cathedral in a magical setting.
- **Discovery Museum** - Find out about life in Newcastle and Tyneside from the area's renowned maritime history and world-changing science and technology right through to fashion through the eras as well as military history.

64. Where to Get Half Price Theatre Tickets in London

Check out the Tkts Half-Price Ticket Booth located in Leicester Square (which is in the heart of Theatreland). This is the place to check for cheap theatre ticket deals before you check anywhere else as they are "official."

There will be many other places that purport to sell half-price tickets, but the one in Leicester Square is run by the actual theaters, and it's where they unload unsold seat inventory, so check there first.

You can also check out the official website at https://www.tkts.co.uk/ for the latest deals.

65. Best Places in London to Hear Free Music

There are many places in London that offer opportunities to hear free music. Here's our list of the best:

- St Martin-in-the-Fields at lunchtime every day
- Covent Garden Market on the lower levels
- Buskers (street performers) on the South Bank of the River
- Southbank Centre
- St James Church in Piccadilly – Free music recitals at 1:10 pm on Mondays, Wednesdays, and Fridays.

66. People Watching is Free!

I f you're short on cash while in Britain and want something to do, people-watching is free!

If you want to just sit around and watch London go by, grab a sandwich and sit on the steps to the National Gallery in Trafalgar Square for some of the best people-watching in London, or check out Hyde Park.

If you're outside London, pick any high street or central business area, and you're bound to be entertained. Most public squares are next to free attractions, so you can take advantage of those as well!

67. Read Local British Newspapers to Discover Stuff!

Wherever you are in Britain, there's still a vibrant local newspaper industry. Pick up a cheap local newspaper, and you're bound to find something free and fun to do while you're there. This is especially useful in London, where newspapers like The Evening Standard have a ton of free and fun things to do in their Friday editions.

So, when in Rome, do as the Romans do and read the local paper. Personally, I like to read local papers just to get a feel for the area and what life is like there. Some of the quirkiest and most interesting events are local matters that don't get much press outside of Britain - or even their county! Reading the local paper is like peeling away a layer of the community and peeking inside. It's a great way to transition from being a tourist to a traveler.

68. Book a Dinner and Theatre Combo Deal

If you're looking for a good deal on a date night in London and want to do a nice dinner and take in a show, consider doing a dinner/theatre combo deal. Often you can get a nice dinner in a restaurant as well as theatre seats, so you get one great night out for one discounted price.

This is a great way to save money on both the dinner as well as the show itself.

Start browsing here:
https://www.londontheatre.co.uk/theatre-breaks

69. Top 5 Free Things to do in Leicester

Leicester is a vibrant and fun city to visit, so we've put together our list of the top 5 sites that you shouldn't miss:

- **Charnwood Museum** - Situated in the pleasant Queen's Park, this museum features permanent exhibitions grouped into four areas: Coming to Charnwood, The Natural World of Charnwood, Living off the Land, and Earning a Living.
- **Gas Museum, National Gas Museum Trust** - The largest museum in the world devoted to gas! Gas appliances and equipment.
- **Leicester Royal Infirmary: History Museum** - Covers the fascinating history of medicine.
- **Belgrave Hall Museum & Gardens** - Stunning home that tells the history of Leicester.
- **Abbey Pumping Station** - This is Leicester's Museum of Science and Technology, displaying its industrial, technological and scientific heritage.

70. Top 5 Free Things to do in Aberdeen, Scotland

Aberdeen is not known for being hot on the tourist trail in Britain, but if you find yourself traveling that far north, there's plenty to see and do on a budget. Here's our list of the top free things to do:

- **Aberdeen Art Gallery** – This splendid gallery houses an important fine art collection with particularly good examples of 19,th 20th and 21st century works, a rich and diverse applied art collection, an exciting program of special exhibitions, a gallery shop, and a café.
- **Aberdeen Maritime Museum** – This award-winning museum tells the story of the city's long relationship with the sea. It's located on the historic Shiprow and incorporates Provost Ross's House, which was built in 1593. The museum houses a unique collection covering shipbuilding, fast sailing ships, fishing, and port history.
- **Provost Skene's House** - Dating from 1545, it now houses an attractive series of period rooms furnished to show how people lived in the 17,th 18th and early 19th centuries. The house is named after one of Aberdeen's most famous residents, Lord Provost George Skene, who is thought to have commissioned the carved plaster ceilings. Visitors can admire an unusual series of religious paintings in the Painted Gallery and enjoy changing displays of dress in the Costume Gallery.
- **Aberdeenshire Farming Museum** - Award-winning portrayal of regional farming history over the past 200 years and Hareshowe working farm.
- **Explore Aberdeen's parks** - Aberdeen has many beautiful parks and gardens that are free to enjoy.

71. Pay Attention to your Coins

If you are traveling to Britain from the United States, one very common mistake that most Americans make, myself included, is not paying attention to the coins you receive as change while you are there. Here in the United States, we usually only pay for items using paper money, so when you go to Britain, you may find yourself doing the same thing. While it is perfectly acceptable to pay there using a paper note, keep in mind that some of the coins there have larger denominations than we do in the United States.

It is easy to throw your coins in your pocket and think of them as spare change, but they include £2 and £1 coins. At the end of the day, all those coins can really add up. When you are handed coins, pay attention to what you are getting back. There can be some real value there.

If you are left with a lot of coins at the end of your trip, a great way to spend them is at the airport. Every time I go, I end up with about £10-15 left from my visit, and I always spend it at the airport. Don't bother to exchange coins back into your normal currency; you'll usually lose horribly on the exchange rate. Go buy a local magazine or a sandwich. If you are still left with some coins, they make wonderful souvenirs too or save them for your next trip!

72. Buying Souvenirs on the Cheap

One of the most expensive aspects of traveling can be souvenir shopping. Just about everyone would love to take home a little something to remind them of their trip, and it seems that every tourist attraction has a shop to buy souvenirs. Many attractions even funnel traffic to exit through the gift shop to entice you. However, if you're a smart shopper, you will save money and have a wonderful souvenir to remember your trip.

My first suggestion is to avoid gift shops at attractions. Museums, historical attractions, and other tourist venues always have gift shops. Most sell gifts that are unique to that specific attraction, and they also sell city souvenirs. For example, at the Tower of London, they sell Tower souvenirs and London souvenirs. Don't buy your city-specific gifts here – they are way overpriced!

Set a budget BEFORE you go into the gift shop. I usually give myself a budget for the day, making sure to include some spending money in case I see something I like. Keeping this in mind, I usually allow one large splurge or expensive souvenir from the trip.

While I do not suggest buying city-specific items at gift shops in popular attractions, there are some gifts that can only be bought there. For example, an art print at a museum or a replica of the crown jewels at the Tower of London. If the souvenir is relevant to the attraction, chances are you aren't going to find it anywhere else, so buy it.

My last suggestion is to shop at the airport. Most large airports, especially when flying internationally, offer duty-free shopping. Avoiding the hefty VAT tax is a huge plus. I always do my souvenir shopping at the airport. Heathrow especially has awesome shopping. I can get all of my Harrods souvenirs at a fraction of the price, and I get all my London gear there, too.

Things to keep in mind: be choosey, shop for price and don't be afraid to splurge at specific attractions. Also, remember that you must travel home with whatever you buy. A fragile souvenir may be a great gift but consider how you are going to get it home. Can you carry it on the airplane? Last but not least, remember that you want something special to remind you of the unique experiences that you've had.

73. Shopping Tip: Don't Buy British DVDs – They Won't Work at Home

D VDs are region-coded, and British DVDs are in a different video format than US TV sets. While most DVD players can convert the video format, you won't be able to play them in America unless you've purchased a "region-free" DVD player.

Most new Bluray DVDs are not region-coded, but this varies by manufacturer. It's better not to take the risk unless you own a region-free DVD player.

Some souvenir shops will sell region-free DVDs aimed at tourists. It's OK to buy these but double-check the packaging. If not, save your money and buy the same DVD when you get home.

CDs are OK to buy.

In the age of streaming, I do realize that this tip is almost worth taking out completely since very few people still buy DVDs, but you can still buy DVDs widely in Britain and there will be many you can't find back home, so a word of warning is valuable!

74. Don't Convert to Dollars at Checkout

A new feature in a lot of stores these days is that when they swipe your American (or foreign) credit card, they'll offer to convert your purchase to dollars on the spot rather than process your purchase in British pounds (and let your credit card do it).

You would think that this would be a better deal for you if you can get the lowest exchange rate – at least that's what these companies want you to think. You won't get a good exchange rate, and the premium you pay just lines the pockets of the store.

When a check out person asks you if you want to convert to dollars, politely decline and have the transaction run in British pounds. In the end, you'll get a better deal. Or if you want an even better deal, just pay cash.

75. Hold on to Your Receipts for a VAT Refund at the Airport

It's no secret that Britain's 20% VAT (or sales tax) hurts when traveling in Britain. It inflates the costs of everything, and you don't notice it because it's built into every price - so things just seem more expensive.

You can, however, get some of the VAT back at the airport when you leave Britain. But you have to do a little legwork to get it.

You need to shop at a retailer that supports the VAT refund scheme, so ask. Most major retailers and department stores will be participating in the program. They'll have to give you a special form that you take with your receipt to the airport.

Once you get to the airport and get through security, find the Customs window and give them all your paperwork. You should get a voucher for a refund at one of the currency exchanges. You may also have to actually have the items with you at the counter. It's a lot of hassle, but if you spent a lot of money shopping while in Britain, it's worth doing.

One special note: you can't claim the VAT back on services like your hotel stay. We tried once. Doesn't work.

76. Hold on to Your Receipts for a VAT Refund at the Airport

Historic Royal Palaces is the independent charity that runs the Tower of London; Hampton Court Palace; Kensington Palace (State Apartments and Orangery); The Banqueting House, Whitehall; Kew Palace with Queen Charlotte's Cottage; and Hillsborough Castle as tourist attractions (and maintains them). This allows HM The Queen to charge tourists for entry into the castles and palaces and then funnel the money to their care. They do very important work.

They also have an overseas membership program. At the time of publication, it costs £55 a year for an individual, £83 for two, £79 for a family. Membership gets you: free unlimited entry to all the castles and palaces; a discount on admission to Kew; subscription to the HRP magazine; 10% off in the gift shops; and an exclusive program of letters and member-only events.

If you plan to visit more than one of these places on your trip to Britain and add up the costs of admission for a family, then the math quickly shows that it's a great deal as you also get to skip the lines (currently you have to book a place in advance). So, for example, for £79 - about $100, my family could get into all of these places - that's a great deal when it would cost almost £100 for us to just go to the Tower of London alone.

77. Shop at Local Markets - Avoid Touristy Markets

You can save a lot of money on food and souvenirs if you shop at local markets in Britain but watch out for markets geared at tourists – where you won't save any money.

Here are two examples:

Borough Market, London - A rich market frequented by locals that offers foods, goods, and more. It's at the top of the list for local markets in London.

Jubilee Market, Covent Garden, London - A market geared toward tourists right off Covent Garden. Locals don't frequent it, and everything is pretty overpriced. The same goes for the Portobello Road Market.

There are markets throughout Britain. Some will be more touristy than others, but you can easily identify them. If there are locals doing their shopping, there's good value for your money. If all you hear is American or foreign accents, you won't.

78. Candy Makes a Great Souvenir for Family Back Home

If you're traveling in Britain on a budget and are looking for the perfect gift for friends and family back home, consider getting them candy.

British candy makes a great souvenir because it's not very expensive, won't get seized by Customs, and in general British candy is tastier than American candy. Flavors are richer, as is the chocolate. It has something to do with humidity.

It's easy to find. You can find it in any grocery or convenience store or even at the airport on your way back home. Pick up some Aero and Mars bars, and consider your friends and family chuffed they'll be getting tasty British candy.

79. Looking for British Books on a Budget? Try Used Bookstores

I love browsing bookstores when I'm in Britain. There are so many interesting books published there that we don't get here in the USA, so I always feel like a kid in a candy store. It's easy to spend too much money on books (and overload my luggage!).

One way to keep things in check while book shopping in Britain is to stick to used bookshops. There's a ton of them in London and Britain's other major cities, and you can usually get the same books in new condition for pennies on the pound. There are charity shops all over Britain, including Oxfam Books, where you can find great books for almost nothing.

I usually avoid the big chains like Waterstones or WH Smith and stick to used book shops. There's also a great used book market under Waterloo Bridge in London.

80. What About Budget Transatlantic Airlines?

This one is tricky to write about. But I felt it was worth a mention. It's tricky because, as I write this in January 2021, there are no budget transatlantic airlines operating right now. They've either all gone bust or have had to shift operations because of the Covid-19 pandemic.

Before the pandemic, there were several - like Norwegian or Wizz Air or Icelandic Air. They operated on the model started by Ryanair or EasyJet, where they'd sell you a dirt cheap seat, but charge you through the nose for everything else - and then it became a game between you and the airline over what you were willing to pay for to make an 8-hour flight tolerable.

While these airlines seemed successful, most of them never made any money, and quite a few went bust. Once the pandemic is over, they are expected to return. Norwegian will probably be back. JetBlue has said they plan to start transatlantic service, as has Ryanair. Whether or not they save you money will depend. Most of the legacy airlines have started to copy their pricing models - sell you the seat dirt cheap then charge for everything else. Even British Airways does this now.

As always, the best way to get a cheap ticket to Britain is to shop around and book far in advance.

81. Duty-Free Shopping at the Airport Isn't Always a Great Deal

While there are some things worth waiting to buy at the airport (eg, cheap souvenirs), we don't really recommend doing a lot of duty-free shopping at the airports in Britain.

Duty-free shopping makes it seem like you're getting a deal as you don't have to pay sales (or VAT) or any other taxes on items you buy while in transit. It's been our experience, though, that prices are still higher than what you'd pay on the high street in Britain.

Even high dollar items like computers and cameras are way more expensive at the airport. I've never really been tempted by any good deals because there aren't any.

Besides, if you're leaving Britain, chances are you've spent all your vacation money enjoying your trip. Why save it for the airport, which is basically a mall that you can't leave once you enter?

82. Top 5 Free Things to do in Edinburgh

If you're lucky enough to be able to venture north and visit the lovely land of Scotland, we've put together a list of the top free things to do in Edinburgh. There's much to do!

- **Museum of Edinburgh** - This is the city's treasure box — a maze of historic rooms crammed full of iconic objects from the capital's past.
- **The Scottish Parliament** - See how government works in Scotland, explore this amazing new building, and take advantage of the free tours. Only open during certain times.
- **Scottish National Gallery and Portrait Gallery** - Explore these world-class art museums with an awesome selection of western art.
- **St Giles' Cathedral** - Standing halfway between Edinburgh Castle and the Palace of Holyroodhouse, the cathedral was founded in the 12th century. Due to its role in Scotland's Reformation history, it is often referred to as the "Cradle of Presbyterianism."
- **The National Museum of Scotland** - You can explore the entire world in this one museum - just reopened after a huge renovation.

83. Top 5 Free Things to do in Brighton

Brighton is Britain's seaside paradise. While it does have a reputation for having London prices, there's still plenty you can do for free to enjoy your time in this resort. Here's our list of free things you can do:

- **Beach** – Brighton's famous beaches are free!
- **Brighton Pier** - One of the most spectacular piers in Britain is free to enter and enjoy.
- **Brighton Museum and Art Gallery** - After a recent renovation, there's a great selection of art in this world-class gallery.
- **Booth Museum of Natural History** - Explore the natural history of Britain and the south coast at this great museum.
- **Do the undercliff walk** - Stretching from Brighton Marina to Saltdean, the impressive undercliff walk is a popular and scenic coastal walk.

84. Top 5 Free Things to Do in Belfast, Northern Ireland

Northern Ireland doesn't have the reputation as a tourist hotspot, but now that their "troubles" have all but gone, there's much rich history to see in Northern Ireland. We thought it would be fun to put together a list of the top five free sites there.

- **Belfast Botanic Gardens** - Occupying 28 acres of south Belfast, the gardens are popular with office workers, students, and tourists.
- **Ulster Museum** - The museum, located in the Botanic Gardens, has around 8,000 square meters of public display space, featuring material from the collections of fine art and applied art, archaeology, ethnography, treasures from the Spanish Armada, local history, numismatics, industrial archaeology, botany, zoology, and geology.
- **Northern Ireland in the Second World War Memorial Building** – Unique memorial dedicated to Northern Ireland's participation in World War II.
- **Armagh County Museum** - The displays focus on the history, natural history, and culture of County Armagh and include archaeological artifacts; historic domestic tools and items; textiles; and costumes including military uniforms, ceramics, natural history, and geology specimens; and railway memorabilia.
- **Giant's Causeway** – A unique geological formation that's steeped in myth and legend.

85. Cheap Phone Calls Home

As I set out to write the second edition of this book, this is one of the things that needed a complete rewrite. How we communicate has completely changed in the 15 years since we wrote the first edition of this book.

We all have smartphones now, and that's how to talk to each other. There's a panoply of apps to keep in touch with people back home. You can Skype, FaceTime, Zoom, WhatsApp, Facebook, etc., to your heart's content and not pay a dime. Video calls! It's like living in the future.

The key, though, is having a data connection for your phone. Most mobile phone carriers will be happy to let you use your phone abroad, but you will pay dearly for it. If this is too expensive, then you will have to rely on free WiFi, which is available pretty much anywhere, to contact those at home.

Never, under any circumstance, use the phone in your hotel to make an international call. You will get quite the sticker shock on the hotel bill at the end of your stay (and that's not a charge you can talk yourself out of). You may be able to make free local calls but check first before you do.

If you have some spare change, it's always fun to make a call from a classic British red phone box. But finding one these days that still works is always a challenge. The ones that do still work most likely take credit cards. It will cost a few dollars to call home.

Now, though, the cheapest way is to use your free hotel WiFi to do it on your smartphone.

86. Saving on Taxis in London and Beyond

If you're not hiring a car and need to get somewhere you can't get to on the bus or by train, you may need to hire a taxi to take you there.

In central London, this is easy. You can easily hail a black taxi on most London streets. But comparatively, black taxis are the most expensive way to get around (but often the best). The mobile apps have taken over the London taxi trade (and in other big cities in Britain). There are black taxi friendly apps that will let you book in advance and pay a set price. Free Now is currently the best app for doing this, but this changes quite often.

Then there is Uber, which is just as popular in Britain as it is everywhere else. Uber will often be half the price of black taxis, but they're not nearly as good. The drivers are not nearly as experienced and just follow the GPS. They have no local knowledge and can sometimes… not be the best drivers. There are other ride-booking apps as well, too many to list.

Outside of London, it gets trickier. But there are apps and booking services that allow you to book a journey in advance and get the best price. In small local towns where there are only one or two taxi drivers, you can usually just ring them and book a journey for a flat rate. This is where dialing the digits can save you money. Apps haven't penetrated here much.

In London, it's best to avoid minicabs, as they're not much better than Uber and can be expensive. However, outside of London, minicabs are often the only option. So, book in advance, get your price set and keep your wits about you, and you'll be fine.

If you really want to save and avoid taxis altogether, then rely on local buses and walking. But this is easier said than done!

87. Smartphone Tips

If you travel to Britain with your smartphone, you may be very excited to be using it on a foreign trip. You have probably even loaded it with useful apps for your trip. Our warning is to be careful how you use it.

International roaming data charges will put you in the poorhouse. We used our smartphone on a trip once after we first got one and returned home to a surprise $1200 phone bill.

If you really want to use your iPhone while in Britain, here's a few tips to follow:

- Only buy apps that store their data locally.
- Turn off international roaming before you leave home.
- Take advantage of free WiFi.
- Buy an international roaming package from your phone carrier.
- Turn off email or anything else that uses Push notifications.
- Avoid using Google Maps. GPS is free, but the data for loading the maps is not. Avoid text messages as they cost a lot more than texts at home.

Your best bet is to just get an international roaming plan from your phone carrier in advance of your trip; then, you can just use your phone as you do at home. My carrier charges $10 a day, and that is worth it to me. You can save a lot more if you have an unlocked phone and get a local pre-paid UK SIM card. But that's now more trouble than it's worth.

88. You Don't Need a Passport Cover

Passport covers look nice, and they're a nice idea. But you don't need one. The main reason being that the US Customs and Border Protection folks will make you take your passport out of it when they're examining it. You will probably have to do the same at the British border as well.

Passport covers can cost a pretty penny, and they're functionally useless. By all means, go ahead and get one if you don't mind constantly taking the passport out of it.

89. Don't Waste Your Money on a Travel Voltage Converter

We fell for this when we first started traveling to Britain. We bought an expensive power/voltage converter for electrical devices. While there may be instances where this is useful, we have never used it and threw it away long ago to free up the luggage space.

Britain does use three-pronged plugs that are different from plugs in the USA or the rest of the world. We recommend picking up a couple of cheap plug adapters at Walmart or Target. They will be all you need.

Most electronic devices can convert the power already. Most computers and laptops do this, and smaller devices all have standard chargers these days anyway. So, learn from our mistake, and don't buy the voltage converter – you just won't need it.

It's also a good idea to go into a 'pound shop' (Britain's equivalent to a dollar store) and pick up £1 USB charging bricks for your smartphone and tablets. This has proven indispensable on multiple trips! You only need to buy them once!

90. Don't Waste Money on an Airplane Charger for Your Laptop or iPad

Years ago, I bought a special charger for my laptop for use on an airplane. It was not cheap. I've never used it. Learn from this mistake.

Most laptops these days have a long battery life. You can get a good amount of use out of them on the plane, so there's usually no need to charge your device in the air.

Many planes now have standard American pronged plugs in the seats, so you don't need special adapters anymore. This can vary by airline and class you're traveling in.

We recommend charging your devices fully before you leave and taking advantage of free plugs in the airport itself. If you really absolutely need to stay charged, you can buy an extra battery or a power pack, and you shouldn't have a problem.

If you're using a device like an iPhone or iPad (which already have long battery life), most airlines are incorporating USB charging ports in their seats as well.

It's also worth picking up an extra 'charging battery' - an extra battery that can charge your phone or computer several times from a single charge. With this, you don't need to use any unknown USB charging at all. They're only a few bucks, and you will get many uses out of them.

91. Top 5 Free Things to do in Coventry

Coventry is at the heart of England and features much rich history and attractions worth a visit. Though much of the city was destroyed during World War II, there's still plenty of heritage in the city center.

- **Take a walk along medieval Spon Street** - Step back in time with a walk down this street, where shops and bars include a local butcher, an art gallery, and the Old Windmill pub.
- **Coventry Transport Museum** - From the penny-farthing to the DeLorean sports car, the museum hosts a history of road transport.
- **Relax in Coventry's peaceful Memorial Park** - The park hosts various events, including the annual Godiva Festival in June.
- **Visit the Herbert Museum and Art Gallery** - The Herbert has undergone a £20 million redevelopment. It's now a major local attraction, which highlights Coventry as a major city for arts and heritage.
- **Coventry Cathedral** - The Gothic cathedral was destroyed during WWII, but the ruins are still there – right next to the gleaming new cathedral that rose from the ashes. Very moving visit!

92. Top 5 Free Things to do in Bournemouth, England

We love Dorset, and one of our favorite cities is Bournemouth. If you're on a budget, there's plenty to see and do for free if you poke around. We've put together a list of the top five things you can do for free:

- **Pier to Pier walk** - Start at either Bournemouth or Boscombe Pier and finish at the other. Enjoy the scenic stroll along the promenade and treat yourself to coffee and cake at one of the many cafés, restaurants, or hotels at either end.
- **Russell-Cotes Art Gallery & Museum** - Visit one of the most important and fascinating museum-houses in England. It holds collections of international status and reflects the Victorian fascination with world cultures.
- **Swim in the Sea** – It's free to swim in the Atlantic Ocean and enjoy Bournemouth's beaches.
- **Bournemouth's Parks & Gardens** - Bournemouth's gardens are split into three areas of Victorian beauty: starting with the Lower Gardens adjacent to the sea and leading to the Central Gardens in the town center, and then the Upper Gardens.
- **Poole Museum (next to Bournemouth)** - Formerly known as the Waterfront Museum, this local history museum situated on the Lower High Street in the Old Town area of Poole is part of the Borough of Poole Museum Service.

93. 5 Free Things to do in Cumbria

The Lake District is one of Britian's most popular tourist areas - and it's very popular with British people themselves. So visiting it can be expensive, and it can be very crowded. While we can't help with the crowds, we can assist you with some free things to do so you don't have to spend all your money having fun in Britain's own version of the Alps.

- **Hill Walking is Free** - Cumbria is famous for its public footpaths and hill walking which, of course, are free. The expansive views are free. They may be crowded, but you can walk wherever you like, and there are plenty of free places to park.
- **Carlisle Cathedral** – The cathedral is the seat of the Anglican Bishop of Carlisle. It was founded as an Augustinian priory and became a cathedral in 1133. It's the second smallest of England's ancient cathedrals. Its notable features include figurative stone carving, a set of medieval choir stalls and the largest window in the

Flowing Decorated Gothic style in England.

- **Ullswater** - If you see one lake on your trip to Cumbria, it should be Ullswater. This deep and expansive body of water is surrounded by things to do, including free beaches. There's also a public footpath that rings the lake (and you can hop on and hop off the steamer boats while you walk it - though they are not free).
- **Castlerigg Stone Circle** - This ancient monument is Cumbria's equivalent to Stonehenge, though on a much smaller scale. I recommend going early when no one is there; it's just you and the sheep and incredible views of the surrounding hills. It's managed by English Heritage, but it's completely free. Just park on the street.
- **Drive through the Hardknott Pass** - This assumes you have a car, and honestly, if you're going to explore Cumbria, you need a car. Public transport is abysmal. The Hardknott Pass is Britain's steepest road and, as you snake up through the Eskdale Pass, you see some incredible landscapes (and worry if your car will fall down into the valley). Once through the Hardknott Pass, you can stop at Hardknott Roman Fort (also free) and pretend you're a Roman on the edge of the world as you glimpse the Irish Sea.

94. Don't Be Afraid to Buy it There

When you pack for your trip, it's tempting to pack every possible thing you will need. This leads to overloaded luggage and sometimes taking things you really didn't need for your stay in Britain. There are several instances where it's perfectly fine to buy it in Britain if you end up needing something you didn't pack.

We mentioned before that Amazon.co.uk is a great way to get something you may have forgotten. But if you don't want to order online, there are plenty of options to buy anything you need cheaply.

First, almost every British high street now has a Pound shop, where everything in the store costs £1. You can usually find tons of essentials there and even things you wouldn't expect to see there. There are also other discount chains like Aldi and Lidl where they sell things cheaply (and are also good sources for cheap food). You can also get cheap stuff at Asda (which used to be owned by Walmart). Most of the 'regular' British retail chains have their own-brand bargain brands; you just have to poke around for them.

If you need toiletries, you can't go wrong with Boots or Superdrug, which are very much like a Walgreens or CVS. But beyond toiletries, you're better off buying those things at other discount retailers. It's also kind of fun to stumble across local shops that aren't chains. In London, down the street from our favorite hotel, is a local 'ironmonger' (hardware store) where we pick up cheap electrical goods that my son loves to build things with when we get home.

When we lost our luggage one time, we had to go into local shops and buy essentials just to get our trip started and, while it was stressful to lose it, it was rather fun to explore and buy the things we needed in an unknown place and learn a little bit of culture we might have otherwise missed.

95. Don't Carry all of your Money with You

Don't carry all of your money on you when out and about. It's a good idea to hide some money in your luggage or in your room. But hide small amounts only! Large amounts should be in the hotel safe. You just want to make sure not to have all of your money in one place!

I would also not carry all your credit cards on you either. You'll be less tempted to spend, and you'll be much safer if something bad happens. If unfortunately you meet a pickpocket, they won't get all your credit cards.

96. Stock up on Camera Memory Cards and Batteries before Leaving

One mistake we made a few years ago was thinking that if we ran out of memory card space on our digital cameras, we could just buy some while in Britain. This was an expensive mistake.

We recommend stocking up on memory cards at home before you depart for Britain. They're cheap these days, so buy more than you think you need so you're not afraid to take as many pictures as your heart desires.

Also, depending on the make and model of your camera, be sure to stock up on plenty of batteries or a spare rechargeable battery. One of our previous cameras used rechargeable batteries. We only had one with us in Britain, and we ran out of a charge in the middle of sightseeing. A replacement in Britain was eye wateringly expensive.

An extra tip. When we did our drive from Land's End to John O'Groats, I forgot to pack the camera charger. I was able to find one on Amazon UK and have it shipped to the hotel the next day.

97. How to Find Free Public Toilets in Britain

Many Americans are shocked to find that when they travel to Britain for the first time a lot of public toilets charge for the privilege of their use. That's not something very commonplace in the USA.

The Brits have their reasons for charging: it keeps the bathrooms cleaner and keeps out undesirables (like drug addicts). But it can be annoying if you're caught short, and you don't have the exact change to pay for access to a loo.

Public toilets are very common in most major tourist areas, but you will pay a fee. Most major train stations now have free bathrooms, so that's good to know as well. Businesses may not have a public restroom, so don't be offended if they tell you that you can't use theirs.

98. How About Avoiding London All Together?

This tip will be controversial, but if you're really looking to travel around Britain on a budget, avoid going to London altogether.

London is one of the world's most expensive cities. Much travel in Britain revolves around it but, if you've been there before and want to see more of Britain, you can skip it. We have taken a couple of trips to Britain that bypassed the city completely.

Most major international airlines fly direct into Birmingham, Cardiff, Manchester, or Edinburgh airports. Rather than land in London, you arrive in the heart of Britain with many options to explore the countryside off the beaten path. Best of all, you don't have to deal with the madness at Heathrow or deal with the expense of just getting out of Heathrow.

99. Top 5 Free Things to do in Plymouth,

Plymouth is full of rich maritime history and is best known as the departure point for the Pilgrims who settled in Massachusetts. So, what better way to enjoy Plymouth than to gather together the Top 5 free things to do if you're in town?

- **Plymouth City Museum and Art Gallery** - The museum's permanent galleries display extensive collections of fine art, human history, and natural history, together with a program of temporary and touring exhibitions each year.
- **St Andrew's Church** - There has been a church on this site for almost 1200 years. During heavy bombing in World War II, the church was left a burnt-out shell but was reconstructed in 1957.
- **HM Naval Base Devonport** - Tour the base and see where today's modern warships are repaired and serviced. Step aboard a warship or nuclear submarine and experience how sailors live and work aboard. Visit the historic sites of the dockyard dating back to Napoleonic times. Tours are free, but you're advised to book ahead.
- **The Barbican & Sutton Harbour (Mayflower port)** – Plymouth's old port area, now a bustling community of specialist shops, craft workshops, and art galleries. The Pilgrim Fathers' departure for the New World is commemorated here at the Mayflower Steps.
- **Waterfront Walkway** – A walk which allows you to explore the history and magnificent setting of the maritime city.

100. Top 5 Free Things to do in Dover

Dover has been the gateway to Britain for thousands of years and, as a result, has a rich and iconic history. The White Cliffs of Dover are a symbol of Britain and it's worth visiting just to see them. Here's our list of the top five free things to do in Dover.

- **Samphire Hoe** - Interesting walks and cycle rides in an amazing place – the best place to view the White Cliffs!
- **White Cliffs** - Spectacular views and miles of stunning cliff top walks.
- **De Bradelei Wharf** - Superb shopping in a maritime setting.
- **Battle of Britain Memorial** - Visit the national memorial to the aircrew who won the Battle of Britain.
- **Western Heights** - Walk around extensive 18th and 19th century fortifications.

101. Don't Forget to Have Fun!

We've written quite a few words on doing Britain on a budget, but I think for our final budget tip, we'll stick to this:

Don't forget to have fun! Having fun doesn't cost a dime!

Don't spend your whole trip counting every penny to the point where you've sucked all joy out of the experience.

Believe me, we've been there. We've been on trips to Britain where we literally ran out of money but, you know what, we still managed to have a good time. And we still keep going back.

The goal of our budget tips guide is to show that, with careful planning and having a wide breadth of knowledge of travel issues you'll face, you can save some serious money while traveling in Britain and still have a great time.

Have fun! Or else, what's the point of even going?

About Anglotopia

Anglotopia.net is the world's largest website for people who love Britain. Founded in 2007, it has grown to be the biggest community of passionate Anglophiles all around the world. With daily updates covering British Culture, History, and Travel, Anglotopia is the place to get your British Fix and learn about all things British! Search for Anglotopia on the Apple App Store and Google Play Store to get daily British stuff on your smartphone.

https://anglotopia.net
https://londontopia.net

CPSIA information can be obtained
at www.ICGtesting.com
Printed in the USA
FSHW021814020421